**Department of the Interior**
**Office of Inspector General**

# AUDIT REPORT

**U.S. Fish and Wildlife Service**
**Wildlife and Sport Fish Restoration**
**Program Grants Awarded to the**
**State of Colorado,**
**Division of Wildlife,**
**From July 1, 2005, Through June 30, 2007**

**Report No. R-GR-FWS-0009-2008**　　　　　　　　**April 2009**

# United States Department of the Interior

**OFFICE OF INSPECTOR GENERAL**
12030 Sunrise Valley Drive, Suite 230
Reston, VA 20191

April 1, 2009

## AUDIT REPORT

Memorandum

To:  Director
U.S. Fish and Wildlife Service

From:  Suzanna I. Park *[signature]*
Director of External Audits

Subject:  Audit on U.S. Fish and Wildlife Service Wildlife and Sport Fish Restoration Program Grants Awarded to the State of Colorado, Division of Wildlife, From July 1, 2005, Through June 30, 2007 (No. R-GR-FWS-0009-2008)

This report presents the results of our audit of costs incurred by the State of Colorado (State), Division of Wildlife (Division), under grants awarded by the U.S. Fish and Wildlife Service (FWS). FWS provided the grants to the State under the Wildlife and Sport Fish Restoration Program (the Program). The audit included claims totaling approximately $44 million on 128 grants that were open during State fiscal years (SFYs) ended June 30 of 2006 and 2007 (see Appendix 1). The audit also covered Division compliance with applicable laws, regulations, and FWS guidelines, including those related to the collection and use of hunting and fishing license revenues and the reporting of program income.

We found that the Division complied, in general, with applicable grant accounting and regulatory requirements. However, we questioned costs totaling $160,329 from charges to the grants for ineligible expenses and unsupported costs, including in-kind (non-cash) contributions. We also found that the Division did not report all program income earned under the grants, did not have adequate controls over equipment, and did not fully address grant objectives and achievements in final performance reports.

We provided a draft report to the FWS for a response. We summarized the Division and FWS responses after each recommendation, as well as our comments on the responses. We list the status of each recommendation in Appendix 3.

Please respond in writing to the findings and recommendations included in this report by June 30, 2009. Your response should include information on actions taken or planned, targeted completion dates, and titles of officials responsible for implementation.

If you have any questions regarding this report, please contact the audit team leader, Mr. Chris Krasowski, or me at 703–487–5345.

cc:  Regional Director, Region 6, U.S. Fish and Wildlife Service

# Introduction

## Background

The Pittman-Robertson Wildlife Restoration Act and the Dingell-Johnson Sport Fish Restoration Act (Acts)[1] established the Wildlife and Sport Fish Restoration Program. Under the Program, FWS provides grants to States to restore, conserve, manage, and enhance their sport fish and wildlife resources. The Acts and federal regulations contain provisions and principles on eligible costs and allow FWS to reimburse States up to 75 percent of the eligible costs incurred under the grants. The Acts also require that hunting and fishing license revenues be used only for the administration of the State's fish and game agency. Finally, federal regulations and FWS guidance require States to account for any income they earn using grant funds.

## Objectives

Our audit objectives were to determine if the Division:

- claimed the costs incurred under the Program grants in accordance with the Acts and related regulations, FWS guidelines, and the grant agreements;

- used State hunting and fishing license revenues solely for fish and wildlife program activities; and

- reported and used program income in accordance with federal regulations.

## Scope

Audit work included claims totaling approximately $44 million on the 128 grants that were open during SFYs 2006 and 2007 (see Appendix 1). We report only on those conditions that existed during this audit period. We performed our audit at Division headquarters in Denver, CO, and visited 6 service centers, 17 State Wildlife Areas (SWAs), 3 fish hatcheries, 1 marina, and 2 State Parks (see Appendix 2). We performed this audit to supplement, not replace, the audits required by the Single Audit Act Amendments of 1996 and by Office of Management and Budget Circular A-133.

## Methodology

We performed our audit in accordance with the "Government Auditing Standards" issued by the Comptroller General of the United States. Those standards require that we plan and perform the audit to obtain sufficient, appropriate evidence to provide a reasonable basis for our findings and conclusions based on our audit objectives. We tested records and conducted auditing procedures as necessary under the circumstances. We believe that the evidence obtained from our tests and

---

[1] 16 U.S.C. §§ 669 and 777, as amended, respectively.

procedures provides a reasonable basis for our findings and conclusions based on our audit objectives.

Our tests and procedures included:

- examining the evidence that supports selected expenditures charged to the grants by the Division;

- reviewing transactions related to purchases, direct costs, drawdowns of reimbursements, in-kind contributions, and program income;

- interviewing Division employees to ensure that personnel costs charged to the grants were supportable;

- conducting site visits to inspect equipment and other property;

- determining whether the Division used hunting and fishing license revenues solely for administration of the Division; and

- determining whether the State passed required legislation assenting to the provisions of the Acts.

We also identified the internal controls over transactions recorded in the labor and license fee accounting systems and tested their operation and reliability. Based on the results of initial assessments, we assigned a level of risk to these systems and selected a judgmental sample of transactions recorded in these systems for testing. We did not project the results of the tests to the total population of recorded transactions or evaluate the economy, efficiency, or effectiveness of Division operations.

## Prior Audit Coverage

On March 8, 2005, we issued "Audit Report on the U.S. Fish and Wildlife Service Federal Assistance Grants Administered by the State of Colorado, Division of Wildlife, from July 1, 2001, through June 30, 2003" (No. R-GR-FWS-0003-2004). We followed up on the status of the 15 recommendations in the report and found that 11 recommendations were not considered implemented. Although FWS Region 6 received documentation regarding implementation of these recommendations, this information has not yet been received by the Department of Interior, Office of the Assistant Secretary for Policy, Management and Budget, which is tracking the implementations. Nevertheless, we found continuing problems with the Division's controls over personal property, which we discuss in the Findings and Recommendations section of this report.

We also reviewed Colorado's Comprehensive Annual Financial Reports for SFYs 2006 and 2007 and the Single Audit Reports for SFYs 2006 and 2007. The reports contained findings related to the payroll approval process and access controls. We examined these areas as part of our audit and found no material exceptions.

# Results of Audit

## Audit Summary

We found that the Division complied, in general, with applicable grant agreement provisions and requirements of the Acts, regulations, and FWS guidance. However, we identified several conditions that resulted in the findings listed below, including questioned costs totaling $160,329. We discuss the findings in more detail in the Findings and Recommendations section.

**Questioned Costs.** We questioned $160,329 in costs and in-kind contributions claimed on four grants. These costs and contributions were ineligible charges to the grants or not supported by adequate documentation.

**Unreported Program Income.** The Division did not report program income earned from selling Habitat Stamps to non-license holders. The Stamps are required to access lands managed with Program funds.

**Personal Property (Equipment) Management Not Adequate to Safeguard Property.** Supervisors responsible for property informally reassigned equipment to staff in other offices but did not always conduct physical inventories. As a result, the Division is not adequately safeguarding property from loss, damage, or theft.

**Questionable Grant Compliance and Performance Reporting.** The final performance reports for three grants did not fully address whether the Division accomplished the grant objectives.

## Findings and Recommendations

### A. Questioned Costs — $160,329

#### 1. Unsupported Payments to a Subgrantee — $112,091

The Division made payments to a subgrantee for design, engineering, construction, and re-vegetation work performed under Grant F-452-D-1. However, the Division was unable to document $224,180 in costs claimed by the subgrantee ($112,091 federal share) by means of invoices or other documentation. The unsupported costs represent 93 percent of the entire grant award.

The Code of Federal Regulations (50 C.F.R. § 80.15) requires all costs to be supported and substantiated by source documents or other records. It also states that allowable costs are limited to those which are necessary and reasonable for accomplishing approved project purposes.

This issue occurred because the Division did not obtain adequate documentation from the subgrantee to support costs claimed under the grant. As a result, we are questioning the federal share of the unsupported costs totaling $112,091.

**Recommendations**

We recommend that FWS:

1. resolve the $112,091 in costs questioned as unsupported, and

2. require the Division to maintain documentation to fully support costs claimed by subgrantees under the grants.

**Division Response**

The Division stated that it concurred with both recommendations and would resolve the unsupported cost by June 30, 2009.

**FWS Response**

FWS officials stated that the Division's comments would be considered in the preparation of the corrective action plan.

**OIG Comments**

Based on the Division and FWS response, additional information is needed in the corrective action plan, including:

- the specific action(s) taken or planned to address the recommendations;

- titles of officials responsible for implementing the actions taken or planned; and

- verification that FWS headquarters officials reviewed and approved of actions taken or planned by the Division.

2. **Ineligible and Unsupported Payments In Lieu of Taxes — $34,261**

The Division made payments in lieu of taxes (PILT) to counties in which it acquired land. These payments, charged to the Operations and Maintenance Grants (FW-46-M-8 and FW-46-M-7), offset property taxes that the counties lost due to their inability to tax State lands. We found that the Division charged a PILT payment totaling $1,401 (federal share $911) to Grant FW-46-M-8. However, because the land related to this payment was not purchased with Program funds, we could not establish a connection to the Operations and Maintenance Grant. This payment was therefore an ineligible cost under the grant.

We reviewed two additional PILT payments of $30,363 (federal share $12,752), charged to Grant FW-46-M-7, and $31,689 (federal share $20,598), charged to Grant FW-46-M-8. Because the Division could not provide us with the funding source of the lands related to those payments, we could not determine whether they were appropriate operations and maintenance charges. Those costs are therefore unsupported.

The Code of Federal Regulations (50 C.F.R. § 80.15) requires all costs to be supported and substantiated by source documents or other records. It also states that allowable costs are limited to those which are necessary and reasonable for accomplishing approved project purposes.

These issues occurred because Division staff did not realize that PILT payments on lands acquired with non-Program funds constituted ineligible costs under the grants. Therefore, the Division did not have adequate procedures in place to review the allowability of PILT expenditures charged to the Program grants. As a result, we are questioning the federal share of unsupported and ineligible costs totaling $34,261, as shown in Table 1.

| GRANT NUMBER | QUESTIONED COSTS (FEDERAL SHARE) | | |
|---|---|---|---|
| | UNSUPPORTED | INELIGIBLE | TOTAL |
| FW-46-M-7 | $12,752 | $0 | $12,752 |
| FW-46-M-8 | 20,598 | 911 | 21,509 |
| TOTALS | $33,350 | $911 | $34,261 |

Table 1. Federal Share of Questioned Costs Related to PILT

## Recommendations

We recommend that FWS:

1. resolve the $34,261 in questioned costs, and

2. require the Division to establish procedures to review the allowability of PILT expenditures charged to the Program grants.

## Division Response

The Division stated that it did not concur with both recommendations. In order to facilitate resolution of the finding, the Division requested that the FWS provide guidance, regulations, or statutes that support the finding for their review.

## FWS Response

FWS officials stated that the Division's comments would be considered in the preparation of the corrective action plan.

### OIG comments

Based on the Division and FWS response, additional information is needed in the corrective action plan, including:

- the specific action(s) taken or planned to address the recommendations;

- targeted completion dates;

- titles of officials responsible for implementing the actions taken or planned; and

- verification that FWS headquarters officials reviewed and approved of actions taken or planned by the Division.

3. **Ineligible and Unsupported In-Kind Contributions — $13,977**

According to Program requirements, States will be reimbursed up to 75 percent of costs incurred to perform projects under the grants. The remaining non-federal ("State's matching") share must be covered by the State. The State's matching share of costs on Grant F-474-D-1, which funded the construction of instream habitat improvements, was partially composed of non-cash ("in-kind") contributions. The in-kind contributions included the value of volunteer labor, donated supplies, and use of equipment owned by other entities. (The Division calculated the value of donated labor and equipment hours by multiplying labor and equipment rates by the hours donated.) We determined that a portion of the in-kind contributions claimed on this grant was unsupported or donated outside the grant period.

Specifically, we found that the Division:

- did not maintain documentation to support labor and equipment rates used to value in-kind contributions received during the grant period;

- claimed the value of 216 hours that volunteers worked on dates prior to the grant period; and

- did not ensure that volunteers completed, certified, and obtained approval on timesheets in a manner similar to Division employees, as required by federal regulations.

The C.F.R. provides the general documentation requirements for in-kind contributions as well as guidance on calculating their value. Under 2 C.F.R. § 225, Appendix A, C.1.j, which outlines basic guidelines on cost principles, costs must be adequately documented to be allowable under federal awards. According to 43 C.F.R. § 12.64(a)(6), in-kind contributions counting towards satisfying a matching requirement must be verifiable from the records of grantees, and the records must show how the value placed on the in-kind contributions was derived. Furthermore, the Special Grant Conditions of Grant F-474-D-1 stated "all costs approved herein incurred by the State prior to the Effective Date are not eligible for reimbursement."

This issue arose because the employees responsible for oversight of this grant were not aware of the in-kind documentation requirements. As a result, the Division overstated the value of its in-kind contributions on Grant F-474-D-1, resulting in $13,977 in questioned costs (federal share), as outlined in Table 2.

| | CLAIMED COSTS | ALLOWABLE COSTS | QUESTIONED COSTS | | |
| --- | --- | --- | --- | --- | --- |
| | | | UNSUPPORTED | INELIGIBLE (OUT OF PERIOD) | TOTAL |
| Federal Share | $64,254 | $50,276 | $12,553 | $1,424 | $13,977 |
| State Share | 32,953 | 25,784 | 6,438 | 731 | 7,169 |
| TOTALS | $97,207 | $76,060 | $18,991 | $2,155 | $21,146 |

**Table 2. Questioned Costs Related to In-Kind Contributions on Grant F-474-D-1**

**Recommendations**

We recommend that FWS:

1. resolve the $13,977 in questioned costs; and

2. ensure the Division trains employees responsible for grant oversight, so that they maintain adequate records to support volunteer time and labor and equipment rates used to calculate the value of in-kind contributions.

**Division Response**

The Division stated that it concurred with both recommendations. The Division submitted a grant amendment to resolve the questioned costs and increased documentation requirements to subgrantees.

**FWS Response**

FWS officials stated that the Division's comments would be considered in the preparation of the corrective action plan.

**OIG Comments**

Based on the Division and FWS response, additional information is needed in the corrective action plan, including:

- the specific action(s) taken or planned to address the recommendations;

- targeted completion dates;

- titles of officials responsible for implementing the actions taken or planned; and

- verification that FWS headquarters officials reviewed and approved of actions taken or planned by the Division.

**B.    Unreported Program Income**

The Division sells two types of Habitat Stamps that convey privileges to hunt, fish, and/or access SWAs, which are managed with FWS grant funds:

- Individuals who do not purchase a hunting or fishing license but wish to visit an SWA must buy a Habitat Stamp for $10 per person.[2]

- Hunters and anglers automatically purchase a Habitat Stamp when they buy a hunting or fishing license.  The cost is $5, and these Stamps are required on the first two licenses purchased in a calendar year.

Because Grants FW-46-M-7 and FW-46-M-8 funded operations and maintenance activities in each of Colorado's SWAs, the $10 Habitat Stamps purchased *apart* from hunting and fishing licenses for access to SWAs constitute program income.  However, the Division did not report this income to FWS, which amounted to $161,063 in SFY2006 and approximately $350,000[3] in SFY2007, for a total of $511,063.  (We determined that revenue from the $5 Habitat Stamps purchased *concurrently* with hunting and fishing licenses should be considered license revenue, in accordance with 50 C.F.R. § 80.4(a)(1),[4] rather than program income.)

A number of federal requirements apply to program income:

- According to 43 C.F.R. § 12.65(b), program income consists of gross income received by a grantee directly generated by a grant-supported activity, or earned only as a result of the grant agreement during the grant period.

---

[2] Youths 18 and under, seniors 65 and over, the mobility impaired, military hospital patients, and Colorado residents who are active duty military personnel stationed outside Colorado but on leave in the state are not required to purchase a Habitat Stamp.

[3] The Division was unable to provide documentation supporting revenue earned from the sale of $10 Habitat Stamps in FY2007.  This figure is therefore an estimate based on discussions with the Division's Fiscal Services Manager.

[4] According to 50 C.F.R. § 80.4(a)(1), license revenues include income from access and recreation fees imposed by the State to hunt or fish for sport or recreation.

- Furthermore, 43 C.F.R. § 12.65(g) requires that program income be deducted from grant outlays, added to the funds committed to the grant agreement, or used to meet the cost sharing or matching requirement.

- The Fish and Wildlife Service Manual, in 522 FW 19, Exhibit 1, Section 1, states that "Examples of income that should be treated as program income include: ...Fees charged by the State fish and wildlife agency...for use of facilities purchased or managed with Federal Assistance funds."

This issue arose because the Division did not consider revenue from the sale of the $10 Habitat Stamps to be program income. Since the income was not deducted from allowable grant costs to determine the net allowable costs of the federal and State shares, the Division might have been reimbursed more than it should have been under these grants.

### Recommendations

We recommend that FWS:

1. determine whether the Division was reimbursed more than it should have been due to the $511,063 in unreported program income for SFYs 2006 and 2007, and if so, determine how to account for the excess reimbursement; and

2. ensure the Division reports program income generated from the sale of Habitat Stamps used solely for access to SWAs.

### Division Response

The Division stated that it concurred with the recommendations and will credit back program income by June 30, 2010.

### FWS Response

FWS officials stated that the Division's comments would be considered in the preparation of the corrective action plan.

### OIG Comments

Based on the Division and FWS response, additional information is needed in the corrective action plan, including:

- the specific action(s) taken or planned to address the recommendations;

- titles of officials responsible for implementing the actions taken or planned; and

- verification that FWS headquarters officials reviewed and approved of actions taken or planned by the Division.

## C.    Personal Property (Equipment) Management Not Adequate to Safeguard Property

Federal regulations require each State to have adequate controls in place to maintain accountability for equipment. To test the Division's controls, we reviewed its inventory management system and selected 87 pieces of equipment, valued at $1,856,470, for visual inspection. Our test showed that the Division did not sufficiently account for equipment purchased with Program funds and license revenue. For instance:

- We were unable to verify the existence or condition of 30 pieces of equipment (23 percent of the items selected for sampling, valued at $426,211), because these items were not maintained at the same location as the individuals responsible for them.

- Three individuals responsible for equipment informed us that they conducted annual inventories by telephone or email rather than through physical inspection due to the distances between their offices and the equipment's location.

- One person responsible for over $18,000 in equipment remarked that he had not seen the equipment in at least 2 years because his staff used it primarily at another site.

In conducting activities funded under the Acts, 50 C.F.R. § 80.18 places responsibility for the accountability and control of all assets with the State. The State must assure the assets serve the purpose for which they were acquired throughout their useful life. Furthermore, State of Colorado Fiscal Rule 1-10 notes that each State agency is responsible for properly accounting for, inventorying, and safeguarding equipment throughout its useful life.

Because the Division assigned responsibility for pieces of equipment to supervisors who did not actually use them, some individuals allocated equipment to their staff stationed at other locations, without requiring them to sign a property receipt or a similar document. For example, two supervisors in the Southwest Regional Office in Durango informally reassigned equipment to employees in Gunnison and Montrose, over 100 miles away. Without maintaining records on the physical movement of property or instituting similar controls, the Division may not be able to safeguard equipment and ensure that it is used for authorized purposes.

We reported a similar condition in our prior audit report (No. R-GR-FWS-0003-2004, Recommendation H) and recommended that the Division establish an accurate inventory database. Therefore, we are repeating the applicable recommendation from that report. This recommendation will be tracked under the resolution process for the prior audit report.

**Repeat Recommendation**

We recommend that FWS require the Division to keep accurate inventory databases of property acquired with Wildlife and Sport Fish Restoration funds, license fees, or other funding sources and to update the inventory timely for additions, deletions, and location changes.

**<u>Division Response</u>**

The Division stated that it partially concurred with the recommendation.

**<u>FWS Response</u>**

FWS officials stated that the Division's comments would be considered in the preparation of the corrective action plan.

**<u>OIG Comments</u>**

The implementation of this recommendation will be tracked under the prior audit report. Accordingly, FWS should send documentation regarding the implementation of this recommendation to the Department of the Interior, Office of the Assistant Secretary for Policy, Management and Budget.

D.    **Questionable Grant Compliance and Performance Reporting**

States are required to submit performance reports to FWS after completion of each Program grant. These reports provide key information to help FWS ensure that States have spent funds appropriately and achieved project goals. We reviewed eight of the Division's performance reports and found that three of them did not meet federal requirements.

The final performance reports for Grants FW-46-M-7 and FW-46-M-8, which funded the operation and maintenance of SWAs:

- did not provide specific, quantified information on grant accomplishments; and

- were nearly identical even though each grant covered a variety of activities in two different SFYs.

Furthermore, the final performance report for Grant F-161-R-16, which funded the installation of aquatic habitat treatments in the Upper Spinney SWA:

- primarily discussed work completed under prior grant segments but did not fully address any of the objectives from Grant F-161-R-16; and

- indicated that the Division performed work at Terryall Creek SWA, even though such work fell outside the scope of the grant agreement.

According to 43 C.F.R. §§ 12.80(b)(2)(i) and (ii), performance reports for each grant should contain a comparison of actual accomplishments to the objectives established for the grant period and the reasons for slippage if the objectives were not met. Furthermore, 522 FW 7.C requires performance reports on operations and maintenance activities to identify and quantify information on the public usage of SWAs, the effects on fish and wildlife populations, and other benefits derived from the grant award. FWS guidance also requires grantees to submit amendments to grant agreements and obtain the Regional Director's approval to add or delete grant projects (522 FW 1.8.A).

These issues arose because the Division did not have a procedure to ensure all performance reports compared actual accomplishments to the grant objectives. Furthermore, with regard to Grants FW-46-M-7 and FW-46-M-8, Division personnel did not have a process in place to collect quantifiable data on operations and maintenance activities occurring on SWAs throughout the State.

As a result, FWS cannot rely on the final performance reports of these three grants to determine whether the Division effectively and appropriately spent $4,396,034 in federal funds (Table 3). This amount represents 18 percent of all funding provided to the Division through the Program grants in SFYs 2006 and 2007.

| Grant Number | Number of Grant Objectives | Number of Inadequately Addressed Objectives | Claimed Costs | Federal Share Claimed |
|---|---|---|---|---|
| FW-46-M-7 | 1 | 1 | $3,987,119 | $1,578,590 |
| FW-46-M-8 | 1 | 1 | 4,282,795 | 2,647,075 |
| F-161-R-16 | 9 | 9 | 227,159 | 170,369 |
| TOTALS | 11 | 11 | $8,497,073 | $4,396,034 |

Table 3. Inadequately Addressed Grant Objectives and Related Claimed Costs

**Recommendations**

We recommend that FWS:

1. determine whether the Division accomplished the grant objectives and effectively spent funds from Grants FW-46-M-7, FW-46-M-8, and F-161-R-16, and if not, recover any funds not spent appropriately; and

2. direct the Division to collect quantifiable data on grant activities and compare actual accomplishments with grant objectives in final performance reports.

**Division Response**

The Division stated that it concurred with the recommendations. The Division would provide additional information to support the accomplishments of grant objectives by June 30, 2009.

**FWS Response**

FWS officials stated that the Division's comments would be considered in the preparation of the corrective action plan.

**OIG Comments**

Based on the Division and FWS response, additional information is needed in the corrective action plan, including:

- the specific action(s) taken or planned to address the recommendations;

- titles of officials responsible for implementing the actions taken or planned; and

- verification that FWS headquarters officials reviewed and approved of actions taken or planned by the Division.

## STATE OF COLORADO
## DIVISION OF WILDLIFE
## FINANCIAL SUMMARY OF REVIEW COVERAGE
## JULY 1, 2005, THROUGH JUNE 30, 2007

| GRANT NUMBER | GRANT AMOUNT | CLAIMED COSTS | QUESTIONED COSTS (FEDERAL SHARE) | | |
| --- | --- | --- | --- | --- | --- |
| | | | UNSUPPORTED | INELIGIBLE | TOTAL |
| F-83-R-19 | $629,470 | $629,470 | | | |
| F-83-R-20 | 670,746 | 670,746 | | | |
| F-86-R-19 | 1,394,936 | 1,394,936 | | | |
| F-86-R-20 | 1,366,969 | 1,366,969 | | | |
| F-161-R-16 | 257,032 | 227,159 | | | |
| F-237-R-13 | 338,370 | 338,370 | | | |
| F-237-R-14 | 365,466 | 335,052 | | | |
| F-239-R-13 | 139,985 | 132,187 | | | |
| F-239-R-14 | 129,295 | 129,295 | | | |
| F-242-R-13 | 130,436 | 130,436 | | | |
| F-242-R-14 | 67,379 | 67,379 | | | |
| F-243-R-13 | 188,606 | 188,606 | | | |
| F-243-R-14 | 240,491 | 240,491 | | | |
| F-288-R-9 | 169,134 | 166,923 | | | |
| F-312-D-10 | 4,389,519 | 4,389,518 | | | |
| F-312-D-11 | 3,798,597 | 3,798,597 | | | |
| F-387-R-6 | 313,628 | 313,628 | | | |
| F-387-R-7 | 434,000 | 363,796 | | | |
| F-394-R-5 | 227,543 | 227,543 | | | |
| F-394-R-6 | 183,594 | 183,594 | | | |
| F-404-D-1 | 40,000 | 23,967 | | | |
| F-415-D-1 | 111,824 | 111,824 | | | |
| F-421-D-1 | 54,260 | 0 | | | |
| F-425-D-1 | 393,336 | 0 | | | |
| F-427-R-3 | 175,710 | 166,132 | | | |
| F-427-R-4 | 176,127 | 171,625 | | | |
| F-428-D-1 | 156,175 | 156,175 | | | |

## STATE OF COLORADO
## DIVISION OF WILDLIFE
## FINANCIAL SUMMARY OF REVIEW COVERAGE
## JULY 1, 2005, THROUGH JUNE 30, 2007

| GRANT NUMBER | GRANT AMOUNT | CLAIMED COSTS | QUESTIONED COSTS (FEDERAL SHARE) | | |
|---|---|---|---|---|---|
| | | | UNSUPPORTED | INELIGIBLE | TOTAL |
| F-429-D-1 | $339,534 | $243,441 | | | |
| F-431-D-1 | 103,111 | 77,873 | | | |
| F-432-D-1 | 108,000 | 90,191 | | | |
| F-433-B-1 | 356,565 | 356,565 | | | |
| F-434-D-1 | 122,872 | 122,872 | | | |
| F-435-D-1 | 184,155 | 184,155 | | | |
| F-436-D-1* | 280,200 | 0 | | | |
| F-437-B-1 | 14,578 | 14,578 | | | |
| F-438-B-1 | 5,000 | 2,354 | | | |
| F-439-B-1 | 554,700 | 554,700 | | | |
| F-440-D-1 | 58,159 | 21,065 | | | |
| F-441-L-1 | 666,675 | 666,625 | | | |
| F-442-D-1* | 63,970 | 27,505 | | | |
| F-443-D-1 | 97,216 | 90,344 | | | |
| F-444-D-1 | 121,500 | 121,500 | | | |
| F-445-D-1 | 55,500 | 55,500 | | | |
| F-446-D-1* | 49,068 | 47,877 | | | |
| F-447-D-1* | 115,000 | 0 | | | |
| F-448-D-1* | 55,225 | 0 | | | |
| F-449-B-1 | 14,759 | 14,759 | | | |
| F-450-B-1 | 178,100 | 178,100 | | | |
| F-451-D-1 | 40,000 | 40,000 | | | |
| F-452-D-1 | 240,000 | 240,000 | $112,091 | | $112,091 |
| F-453-D-1 | 124,530 | 124,530 | | | |
| F-454-DB-1 | 377,392 | 0 | | | |
| F-455-D-1 | 69,000 | 69,000 | | | |
| F-456-B-1 | 35,885 | 35,885 | | | |
| F-457-B-1 | 150,675 | 150,675 | | | |
| F-458-B-1* | 120,889 | 46,075 | | | |
| F-459-B-1 | 4,278 | 4,061 | | | |
| F-460-B-1* | 122,507 | 81,014 | | | |
| F-461-D-1* | 439,675 | 0 | | | |

## STATE OF COLORADO
## DIVISION OF WILDLIFE
## FINANCIAL SUMMARY OF REVIEW COVERAGE
## JULY 1, 2005, THROUGH JUNE 30, 2007

| GRANT NUMBER | GRANT AMOUNT | CLAIMED COSTS | QUESTIONED COSTS (FEDERAL SHARE) | | |
| --- | --- | --- | --- | --- | --- |
| | | | UNSUPPORTED | INELIGIBLE | TOTAL |
| F-462-D-1* | $177,450 | $0 | | | |
| F-463-D-1* | 17,000 | 17,000 | | | |
| F-464-D-1* | 27,000 | 0 | | | |
| F-465-D-1* | 71,500 | 0 | | | |
| F-466-D-1* | 53,500 | 53,008 | | | |
| F-467-D-1* | 30,325 | 0 | | | |
| F-468-D-1* | 240,000 | 0 | | | |
| F-469-B-1* | 66,000 | 0 | | | |
| F-470-B-1* | 210,438 | 0 | | | |
| F-471-B-1* | 116,468 | 0 | | | |
| F-472-B-1* | 120,208 | 0 | | | |
| F-473-D-1* | 60,000 | 23,675 | | | |
| F-474-D-1* | 118,000 | 97,207 | $12,553 | $1,424 | $13,977 |
| F-475-B-1 | 205,010 | 201,000 | | | |
| F-476-B-1 | 25,626 | 25,375 | | | |
| F-477-B-1 | 36,825 | 27,104 | | | |
| F-478-D-1* | 125,000 | 0 | | | |
| F-480-B-1 | 6,465 | 6,465 | | | |
| F-481-B-1* | 85,250 | 9,209 | | | |
| F-482-B-1* | 30,576 | 25,143 | | | |
| F-483-B-1 | 4,510 | 4,510 | | | |
| F-485-B-1 | 1,340,000 | 0 | | | |
| F-486-B-1 | 33,250 | 33,250 | | | |
| F-487-B-1* | 35,500 | 8,993 | | | |
| F-488-B-1* | 13,319 | 13,319 | | | |
| F-489-D-1 | 112,000 | 0 | | | |
| F-490-B-1* | 17,734 | 11,181 | | | |
| F-491-B-1* | 89,160 | 89,160 | | | |
| F-492-B-1* | 49,905 | 0 | | | |
| F-493-D-1 | 238,000 | 0 | | | |
| F-494-B-1 | 100,216 | 0 | | | |
| F-495-D-1 | 247,311 | 0 | | | |

## STATE OF COLORADO
## DIVISION OF WILDLIFE
## FINANCIAL SUMMARY OF REVIEW COVERAGE
## JULY 1, 2005, THROUGH JUNE 30, 2007

| GRANT NUMBER | GRANT AMOUNT | CLAIMED COSTS | QUESTIONED COSTS (FEDERAL SHARE) | | |
| --- | --- | --- | --- | --- | --- |
| | | | UNSUPPORTED | INELIGIBLE | TOTAL |
| F-496-D-1* | $36,000 | $0 | | | |
| F-497-B-1* | 172,700 | 0 | | | |
| F-498-D-1 | 132,000 | 0 | | | |
| F-499-D-1 | 158,000 | 0 | | | |
| F-500-D-1 | 40,000 | 0 | | | |
| F-501-D-1 | 85,900 | 0 | | | |
| F-502-D-1 | 17,000 | 0 | | | |
| F-503-B-1* | 8,930 | 0 | | | |
| F-504-D-1 | 195,000 | 0 | | | |
| F-505-B-1* | 10,000 | 0 | | | |
| F-506-D-1 | 20,000 | 0 | | | |
| F-507-D-1 | 308,808 | 0 | | | |
| F-508-B-1* | 6,000 | 0 | | | |
| FW-28-T-19 | 1,291,726 | 1,088,611 | | | |
| FW-28-T-20 | 973,309 | 897,509 | | | |
| FW-31-P-19 | 1,459,513 | 1,322,022 | | | |
| FW-31-P-20 | 1,155,833 | 1,092,403 | | | |
| FW-45-L-7 | 804,809 | 697,573 | | | |
| FW-45-L-8 | 794,455 | 702,914 | | | |
| FW-46-M-7 | 4,106,734 | 3,987,119 | $12,752 | | $12,752 |
| FW-46-M-8 | 4,282,795 | 4,282,795 | 20,598 | $911 | 21,509 |
| FW-47-C-2 | 257,419 | 227,855 | | | |
| FW-47-C-3 | 268,548 | 268,548 | | | |
| W-148-E-19 | 1,484,272 | 2,566,282 | | | |
| W-148-E-20 | 1,051,767 | 1,051,767 | | | |
| W-182-R-6 | 852,245 | 678,302 | | | |
| W-182-R-7 | 938,685 | 895,620 | | | |
| W-183-R-6 | 1,277,316 | 1,173,292 | | | |
| W-183-R-7 | 1,342,086 | 1,342,086 | | | |
| W-185-R-5 | 446,831 | 400,564 | | | |
| W-185-R-6 | 448,482 | 448,482 | | | |
| W-186-E-1 | 499,000 | 499,000 | | | |

**STATE OF COLORADO
DIVISION OF WILDLIFE
FINANCIAL SUMMARY OF REVIEW COVERAGE
JULY 1, 2005, THROUGH JUNE 30, 2007**

| GRANT NUMBER | GRANT AMOUNT | CLAIMED COSTS | QUESTIONED COSTS (FEDERAL SHARE) | | |
| --- | --- | --- | --- | --- | --- |
| | | | UNSUPPORTED | INELIGIBLE | TOTAL |
| W-186-E-2* | $343,074 | $58,685 | | | |
| W-186-E-3 | 7,500 | 3,828 | | | |
| W-186-E-4 | 24,454 | 24,432 | | | |
| W-186-E-5 | 277,600 | 0 | | | |
| W-187-E-1* | 65,000 | 0 | | | |
| TOTALS | $51,558,683 | $43,940,950 | $157,994 | $2,335 | $160,329 |

*Because grant periods did not always correspond with the State fiscal year, the Division of Wildlife had not submitted SF-269s for these 36 grants for the period ending June 30, 2007. We therefore used the net payments from the FWS iFAIMS to determine Claimed Costs.

### STATE OF COLORADO
### DIVISION OF WILDLIFE
### SITES VISITED

#### Headquarters

Denver

#### Service Centers

Durango
Meeker
Monte Vista
Northwest Region (Grand Junction)
Salida
Southwest Region (Durango)

#### State Wildlife Areas

63 Ranch
Badger Basin
Bel Aire
Billy Creek
Bodo
Dan Noble
Dry Creek Basin
Garfield Creek
Jerry Creek Reservoir
Lake Avery
Nelson/Prather Easement
Oak Ridge
Pastorius Reservoir
Perins Peak
Plateau Creek
Spinney Mountain
White River

## Fish Hatcheries

Mt. Shavano
J.W. Mumma Native Aquatic Species Restoration Facility
Rifle Falls

## Other Sites Visited

Frisco Bay Marina
Navajo State Park
Rifle Gap State Park

**STATE OF COLORADO**
**DIVISION OF WILDLIFE**
## STATUS OF AUDIT FINDINGS AND RECOMMENDATIONS

| Recommendations | Status | Action Required |
|---|---|---|
| **A.1.1, A.1.2, A.2.1, A.2.2, A.3.1, A.3.2, B.1, B.2, D.1 and D.2** | FWS acknowledges the recommendations but additional information is needed as outlined in the "Action Required" column. | Additional information is needed in the corrective action plan, including: the specific action(s) taken or planned to address the recommendations, targeted completion dates, titles of officials responsible for implementing the actions taken or planned; and verification that FWS headquarters officials reviewed and approved of actions taken or planned by the Division. We will refer recommendations not resolved and/or implemented at the end of 90 days to (after June 30, 2009) to the Assistant Secretary for Policy, Management and Budget (PMB), for resolution and/or tracking of implementation. |
| **C** | Repeat recommendation H from our prior report (R-GR-FWS-0003-2004) PMB considers this resolved but not implemented. | Provide documentation regarding the implementation of this recommendation to PMB. |

# <u>Report Fraud, Waste, Abuse,</u>
# <u>and Mismanagement</u>

Fraud, waste, and abuse in government
concerns everyone: Office of Inspector
General staff, Departmental employees,
and the general public. We actively
solicit allegations of any inefficient and
wasteful practices, fraud, and abuse
related to Departmental or Insular Area
programs and operations. You can report
allegations to us in several ways.

**By Mail:**     U.S. Department of the Interior
Office of Inspector General
Mail Stop 4428 MIB
1849 CStreet, NW
Washington, D.C. 20240

**By Phone:**   24-Hour Toll Free        800-424-5081
Washington Metro Area    703-487-5435

**By Fax:**     703-487-5402

**By Internet:**   www.doioig.gov/hotline

www.ingramcontent.com/pod-product-compliance
Lightning Source LLC
Chambersburg PA
CBHW080403290526
45790CB00009BA/3685